is due fo ... date shown below.

EXPLORE Geography

Analysing geographical data

Catherine Yemm

Heinemann

www.heinemann.co.uk/library
Visit our website to find out more information about **Heinemann Library** books.

To order:
 Phone 44 (0) 1865 888066
 Send a fax to 44 (0) 1865 314091
 Visit the Heinemann Bookshop at www.heinemann.co.uk/library to browse our catalogue and order online.

First published in Great Britain by Heinemann Library, Halley Court, Jordan Hill, Oxford OX2 8EJ, part of Harcourt Education. Heinemann is a registered trademark of Harcourt Education Ltd.

© Harcourt Education Ltd 2006
The moral right of the proprietor has been asserted.

Editorial: Vicki Yates
Design: Dave Poole and Tokay Interactive Limited (www.tokay.co.uk)
Illustrations: Geoff Ward and International Mapping (www.internationalmapping.com)
Picture Research: Hannah Taylor
Production: Duncan Gilbert

Originated by Repro Multi Warna
Printed in China by WKT Company Limited

10 digit ISBN: 0 431 03257 2   (Hardback)
13 digit ISBN: 978 0 431 03257 3   (Hardback)
10 09 08 07 06
10 9 8 7 6 5 4 3 2 1

10 digit ISBN: 0 431 03264 5   (Paperback)
13 digit ISBN: 978 0 431 03264 1   (Paperback)
10 09 08 07 06
10 9 8 7 6 5 4 3 2 1

British Library Cataloguing in Publication Data
Yemm, Catherine
Analysing geographical data
910.2'85
A full catalogue record for this book is available from the British Library.

Acknowledgements
The publishers would like to thank the following for permission to reproduce photographs:
Alamy Images p. **4** (Photofusion Picture Library), p. **6** (Dominic Burke), p. **7** (Emmanuel Coupe), p. **18** (tradewinds), p. **20** (David Wall), p. **28** (Ian Shaw), p. **29** (eStock Photo); BBC p. **22**; Corbis p. **10** (LWA-JDC), p. **19** (ZUMA/ Kelly Owen), p. **21** (Ashley Cooper/PICIMPACT); Empics p. **24** (Peter Jordan), p. **27** (PA/Yul Mok); Getty Images p. **12** (Taxi); Harcourt Education Ltd p. **25** (Tudor Photography); Imray, Laurie, Norie and Wilson Ltd, Reproduced by permission of The Controller of Her Majesty's Stationery Office and the UK Hydrographic Office p. **13**; PA weather centre p. **23**; Press Association p. **11**; Reproduced by permission of Ordnance Survey on behalf of The Controller of Her Majesty's Stationery Office, © Crown Copyright 100000230 p. **15**; Science Photo Library p. **16** (WORLDSAT INTERNATIONAL), p. **17** (Digital Globe, Eurimage); Thame Gazette p. **26**.

Cover photograph of a meteorologist attending to a Doppler weather radar, reproduced with permission of Corbis/Brownie Harris.

The publishers would like to thank Rebecca Harman, Rachel Bowles, Robyn Hardyman, and Caroline Landon for their assistance in the preparation of this book.

Exploring further

Throughout this book you will find links to the Heinemann Explore CD-ROM and website at www.heinemannexplore.com. Follow the links to find out more about the topic.

Contents

Statistical data

Collecting statistical data   4

Analysing statistical data   6

Communicating statistical data   8

Using statistical data   10

Mapping data

How do we use mapping data?   12

Analysing mapping data   14

Photographic data   16

Weather data

How do we analyse weather data?   18

Using weather data   20

What will the weather be like today or tomorrow, here and around
the world?   22

Media data

How do we analyse media data?   24

What is in the newspapers today?   26

Communicating your data   28

Glossary   30

Find out more   31

Index   32

Any words appearing in the text in bold, **like this**, are explained in the glossary.

Statistical data

Collecting statistical data

Geographical **data** helps us to find out more about the world around us. Data tells us about the area we live in and how that area is changing, or can be changed. Data is information that can be collected, **analysed**, communicated, and used. For example, traffic data can tell us how many cars are on our roads. This data can be used to help reduce traffic jams.

When it is in the form of numbers, data is called **statistics**. It can also be presented in other forms, such as in maps, **atlases**, and photographs. Below are some of the ways in which we can collect statistical data.

Asking questions

Asking people to answer questions can provide statistics. In order for the statistics to be useful, you need to ask a lot of people the same questions and compare their answers. For example, to gather statistics on how people get to school each morning, you need to ask as many people as possible. They may tell you that they walked, cycled, or were driven by car. You need to record their answers.

■ *A **census** provides the **government** with statistics about the people in the UK.*

Observing and counting

Observing something and counting it when it happens can also provide us with statistics. Sometimes it is easier to observe and count things than it is to ask questions. For example, if you want to collect data on the number of people who travel into your town each morning, it will take a long time to ask everybody how they intend to go into town. It is much easier to count the people actually entering the town.

cars	vans	bikes
~~IIII~~	III	II
IIII		
II		

- *When collecting data in this way, it is important to use some form of chart to help you keep count. If the data collected is not accurate, the statistics you get from it will not be useful.*

See for yourself

Go out into your street and observe how many cars, bikes, and vans pass you in 15 minutes. Use a chart to record your data.

Analysing statistical data

Once statistical **data** has been collected, it needs to be **analysed**. This is normally done by people called **statisticians**. They do **calculations** with the data. When the statistics have been analysed, the data will be able to tell us things and will not just be a lot of numbers. For example, data on traffic flow can tell us if traffic calming measures are needed.

Sorting out the data

If we group similar types of statistical data together, it often makes them easier to understand. For example, if we were looking at the data on the number of people who travel into town each morning, we would group the number of people who drive in by car, the people who walk in, and the people who ride a bike, or who drive a lorry. The people who come in a car can then be sorted by the number of people in each car. We can then answer questions about how people come into town, and the numbers of different vehicles they use.

If similar information has been gathered in the past, the old and new information can be compared and we can look for **patterns**. Doing this can reveal useful information.

■ *By looking for patterns we might find that every year the number of people cycling into town increases, while the number of people driving in decreases.*

Using the data to predict what will happen

After data has been collected, it is often possible to analyse the data in a way that will help to **predict** what may happen in the future. We may need to collect data for a number of years to be able to do this. By plotting the data on **graphs** and charts we can see if there are any patterns.

- *If the amount of land being **eroded** from the coast has been the same each year for the last five years, we would predict that the same amount will be eroded this year. If the amount had increased by 5 cm (2 inches) each year, we would predict that it would increase by another 5 cm (2 inches) this year.*

Communicating statistical data

Once statistical **data** has been **analysed**, it is usually put into **graphs** and charts to make it easier to understand and to help us to see any **patterns**.

It is important to choose the right type of graph or chart for communicating your data. Different graphs are used for different purposes.

Types of charts and graphs

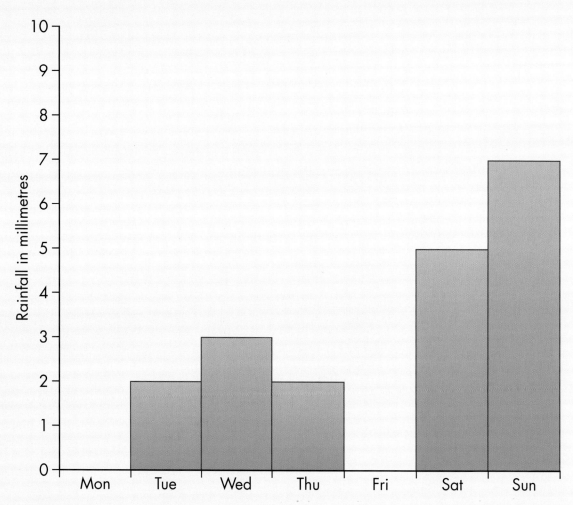

- A **bar chart** is divided into columns that show how things are related. Bar charts are good for displaying results that are not continuous. For example, on a bar chart of how much rain has fallen over a week, it is easy to compare how much rain fell on Monday with how much fell on Friday.

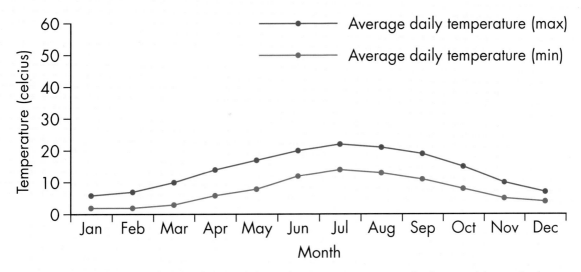

- **Line graphs** are normally used to display data that is continuous. The line on this graph shows how the average temperature in London changes over the year.

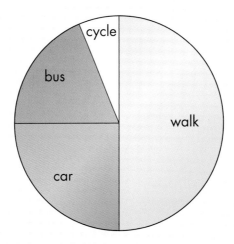

- A **pie chart** is a circle divided into sections. Each section shows a portion of the whole amount. This pie chart shows how 30 children got to school today.

Activity

1 Conduct a **survey** in your class to find out about people's favourite leisure activities.

2 Make a table of your results.

3 Make a graph to display the data. Choose the best kind of graph for the job. Remember to give it a title.

4 Use the **statistics** to help you decide on the best place to go for a school trip.

Using statistical data

Data that has been collected and **analysed** can be used in many different ways: to learn more, to improve things, and to be successful.

How does the government use statistics?

People in **government** use **statistics** to see how well the country is being organized, and to keep track of any changes happening. They use the statistics to decide what jobs need to be done and where to spend their money. **Surveys** help the government to understand the public's views and what the public would like them to do.

One important survey carried out by the government is the **census**. Every ten years all adults in the UK have to answer questions about their family, their house, their work, and their health. All the census forms are handed in to the government. They collect all the answers together and analyse them. This gives them a lot of interesting statistics about the people in the UK and how they live.

■ *Statistics can be studied and used to make things better for everyone.*

How are statistics used in newspapers?

Statistics are often published in newspapers. They may be used in a report to give the reader more information, or to inform people about the results of a survey or an investigation that has been carried out. A good example of statistics that appear in newspapers regularly are the football league tables. The tables are put together using the results of all the football matches that have taken place.

Premiership

	P	Home W	D	L	F	A	Away W	D	L	F	A	GD	Pts	Next three games
▶ Chelsea	6	3	0	0	7	0	3	0	0	5	0	+12	18	Aston Villa (h) 24/9, Liverpool (a) 2/10, Bolton (h) 15/10
▶ Charlton	5	1	0	1	1	2	3	0	0	7	1	+5	12	West Brom (a) 24/9, Tottenham (h) 1/10, Fulham (h) 17/10
▲ Man Utd	5	1	1	0	2	1	2	1	0	4	0	+5	11	Blackburn (h) 24/9, Fulham (a) 1/10, Sunderland (a) 15/10
▲ Bolton	6	1	1	1	2	1	2	1	0	5	3	+3	11	Portsmouth (h) 24/9, Wigan (a) 2/10, Chelsea (a) 15/10
▼ Man City	6	1	1	1	2	2	2	1	0	5	3	+2	11	Newcastle (a) 24/9, Everton (h) 2/10, West Ham (h) 16/10
▲ West Ham	5	2	0	1	8	3	1	1	0	2	1	+6	10	Arsenal (h) 24/9, Sunderland (a) 1/10, Man City (a) 16/10
▼ Tottenham	6	1	1	1	2	2	1	2	0	3	1	+2	9	Fulham (h) 26/9, Charlton (a) 1/10, Everton (h) 15/10
▶ Middlesbrough	6	1	1	1	2	4	1	1	1	4	3	-1	8	Sunderland (h) 25/9, Aston Villa (a) 2/10, Portsmouth (h) 15/10
▲ Wigan	5	1	1	1	2	2	1	0	1	2	2	0	7	Everton (a) 24/9, Bolton (h) 2/10, Newcastle (h) 15/10
▼ Arsenal	4	2	0	0	6	1	0	0	2	1	3	+3	6	Everton (h) 19/9, West ham (a) 24/9, Birmingham (h) 2/10
▶ Liverpool	4	1	1	0	1	0	0	2	0	0	0	+1	6	Birmingham (a) 24/9, Chelsea (h) 2/10, Blackburn (h) 15/10
▲ Aston Villa	6	1	2	0	4	3	0	1	2	1	6	-4	6	Chelsea (a) 24/9, Middlesbro' (h) 2/10, Birmingham (a) 16/10
▲ Portsmouth	6	0	2	1	2	4	1	0	2	3	4	-3	5	Bolton (a) 24/9, Newcastle (h) 1/10, Middlesbrough (a) 15/10
▲ Newcastle	6	0	2	1	1	3	1	0	2	3	4	-3	5	Man City (h) 24/9, Portsmouth (a) 1/10, Wigan (a) 15/10
▼ Fulham	6	1	1	1	2	2	0	1	2	3	7	-4	5	Tottenham (a) 26/9, Man Utd (h) 1/10, Charlton (a) 17/10
▶ Birmingham	6	0	0	3	1	6	1	2	0	4	3	-4	5	Liverpool (h) 24/9, Arsenal (a) 2/10, Aston Villa (h) 16/10
▶ West Brom	6	1	0	2	5	6	0	2	1	1	5	-5	5	Charlton (h) 24/9, Blackburn (a) 1/10, Arsenal (h) 15/10
▼ Blackburn	6	1	1	1	2	4	0	1	2	1	4	-5	5	Man Utd (a) 24/9, West Brom (h) 1/10, Liverpool (a) 15/10
▼ Everton	4	0	0	2	0	3	1	0	1	1	1	-3	3	Arsenal (a) 19/9, Wigan (h) 24/9, Man City (a) 2/10
▶ Sunderland	6	0	1	2	3	6	0	0	3	0	4	-7	1	Middlesbrough (a) 25/9, West Ham (h) 1/10, Man Utd (h) 15/10

- *Newspapers often make use of statistics in their articles, particularly in the sports section.*

Activity

1 Look through a selection of newspapers.
2 How many articles can you find that show tables, **graphs**, or have statistics in the written report?

Don't forget to look in the business and sport sections.

Mapping data

How do we use mapping data?

We can use maps to find places, plan journeys, or learn more about an area. A **key** explains the symbols used on the map, and the **scale** of the map shows how big the area is.

■ *We can plan journeys by studying a map before we set off. We decide which roads we are going to travel on.*

Atlases

An **atlas** is a book of maps or charts that show roads, rivers, lakes, mountains, and many other features. At the back of an atlas is an index, so you can find the right page for the place you are looking for. The front of the atlas has the key and the scale for the maps. The squares across the maps are known as **grid squares**. They are labelled with numbers and letters, so that you can find a place easily.

Activity

1 Look up Musselburgh in the index of your atlas.

2 Find where it is on the map.

3 Use the scale to work out roughly how far it is from where you live.

4 Use maps and atlases to plan a journey between Brighton and Newcastle.

Charts

Maps of the sea and air are often called charts. There are fewer features in the air or sea than on land, but it is still possible to make maps of them so that pilots and sailors can follow a certain path or find a particular place.

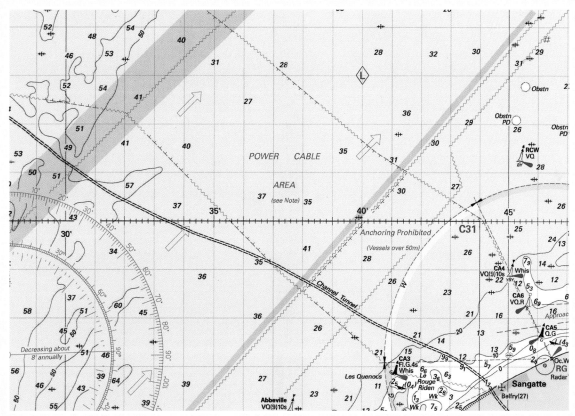

■ *This map of the sea can be used by sailors for **navigation**.*

Keeping up to date

Every year new buildings and roads are built. Even the shape of the land and sea change slightly over time. New maps have to be made to give us the most up-to-date information.

Analysing mapping data

When using a map to **analyse data** it is important to choose the right kind of map for your needs. There are several different kinds of map, including:

- **political maps**, showing the borders between different countries
- **physical maps**, displaying the physical features of the land, such as mountains and rivers
- **climate maps**, showing the climate of a region
- maps of the sea and air that used for **navigation**.

Large scale

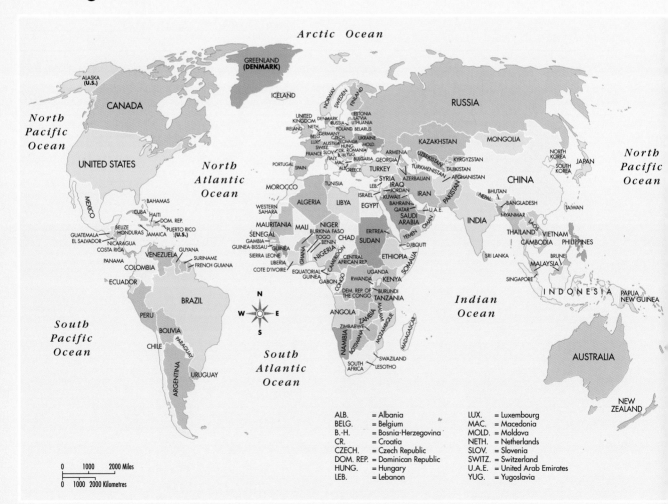

ALB. = Albania
BELG. = Belgium
B.-H. = Bosnia-Herzegovina
CR. = Croatia
CZECH. = Czech Republic
DOM. REP. = Dominican Republic
HUNG. = Hungary
LEB. = Lebanon

LUX. = Luxembourg
MAC. = Macedonia
MOLD. = Moldova
NETH. = Netherlands
SLOV. = Slovenia
SWITZ. = Switzerland
U.A.E. = United Arab Emirates
YUG. = Yugoslavia

■ *To analyse data from a very large area, such as the whole world, you need to look at a map with a large* **scale**. *A map of this scale might include labels for countries,* **capital cities**, *and features such as major rivers and mountains. This is a large-scale political map of the world.*

Small scale

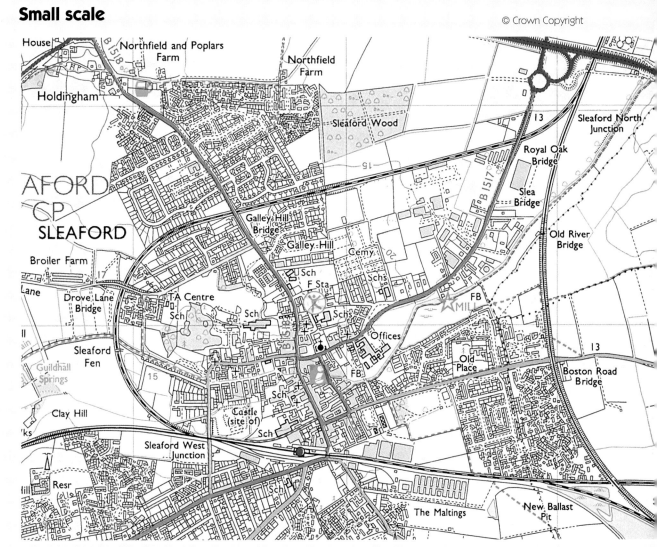

- To analyse data about towns and villages, you need to look at a map with a small scale, such as this Ordnance Survey map. It shows features such as buildings, railway stations, rivers and even the height of the land. With these maps you can analyse data about the types of buildings in an area, the facilities available, and the way the land is used.

See for yourself

You are going to make a map of the grounds and buildings at your school.

1 Walk around your school and collect information about its features. Take some measurements if you think this will help.

2 What sort of scale would be best for your map?

3 Will you need a **key** to explain the features?

4 Can you use different colours to help you explain things more clearly?

Photographic data

Photographs can give us a lot of information. There are several different types of photograph that can be taken depending on the sort of **data** that you want to collect.

Types of photographic data

Still photographs catch an image at one particular moment. They are a good way to collect a lot of detail about a small area. Changes in an area can be recorded by taking a second photograph from the same place where an earlier photograph was taken. Using a video camera to take moving pictures is a good way to collect information about an event that is happening. You can also do this with a **satellite photograph**.

See for yourself

Go into a garden and take a still photograph of part of it. It could be of just one tree or an area of plants. Print the photo, or have it developed. Label your photograph to show what everything is. If you looked at the photograph again in a few months time and compared it with the garden, you would see that the garden has changed.

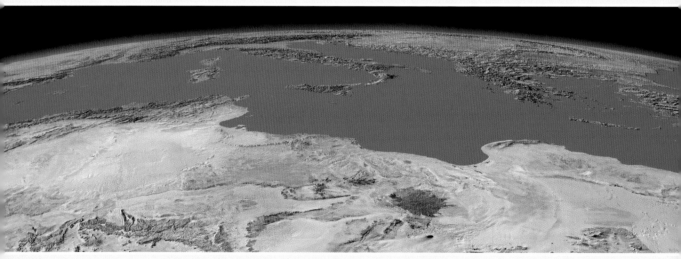

■ *Satellite images are photographs taken from space. They are the best type of photograph for collecting information about a very large area. They can cover a huge area, as this image of North Africa shows.*

Analysing photographic data: time and place

Photographs can tell us that something has happened. They can also tell us when and where something has happened. If there are people in a picture, you might be able to work out when the picture was taken from the style of their clothes. The background of the photograph might help you to work out where the picture was taken.

Analysing photographic data: changes

Comparing pictures of the same area can help you to see changes that have taken place. For example, the information in the satellite pictures below show the terrible flooding caused by Hurricane Katrina in New Orleans.

■ *Satellite picture of New Orleans before Hurricane Katrina hit in 2005.*

■ *This satellite picture shows the same place as the image above. It was taken after Hurricane Katrina hit. You can see that the area is flooded and that most of the roads have diappeared.*

Analysing photographic data: events

Photographs can capture information about an event that has taken place. For example, photographs of a **drought** can reveal the terrible conditions of the people living through it, and some of the pain and fear they are feeling.

Weather data

How do we analyse weather data?

Data about the weather is collected from **weather stations**. Weather instruments are used to measure these aspects of the weather:

- rainfall: the amount of rain that falls
- **temperature**: how hot or cold the air is
- **humidity**: how much water vapour there is in the air
- **air pressure**: the pressure at the surface of the Earth, caused by the weight of the air
- wind strength: how strongly the wind is blowing
- wind direction: the way the wind is blowing, from the north, south, east, or west.

This data is collected at regular times by computers, which plot it on to data charts. These charts are then used to **analyse** the data and so to **predict** the weather in future.

■ *This weather station constantly records weather data.*

Computers

Computers are used to analyse weather data that has been collected all over the world. They use it to produce **models** of the weather. These models show what could happen to the weather in the next few days. **Meteorologists** are people who study the weather. They examine the different models and decide which one is most likely to happen. They use this information to produce a **weather forecast** for the next few days.

■ *Meteorologists use weather data to forecast what the weather will be like.*

Activity

Make your own weather forecast by analysing the data you collect in class.

1 Use a **thermometer** to record the temperature in the playground at 10:00 a.m. every day for three weeks. Keep accurate records of all the data you collect.

2 Use a **rain gauge** to measure the rainfall at the same time every day. Ten days without rain is called a **drought**.

3 Use this data to make a **line graph** for temperature and a **bar chart** for rainfall.

4 Display your results and look for **patterns** in the data.

5 Use your data and your understanding of different types of weather to try to predict the weather for a few days ahead.

6 Collect the weather forecasts from a daily newspaper. Do you agree with them?

7 When the days have passed, look at how accurate your predictions were.

Exploring further

Go to the Heinemann Explore website or CD-ROM, click on Resources > Weather. Now watch the videos showing a weather station and a **radar** tracking rain. Think about how a meteorologist would use this kind of data.

Using weather data

Weather **data** can help us in our everyday lives. If the weather is going to be very hot or very cold, we can plan to wear clothing that will keep us comfortable.

Weather forecasts also help people in their jobs. Builders often look at weather forecasts to know if they will be able to complete the work they have planned. Supermarkets and shops use forecasts to plan the goods they will stock. In cold weather people use more energy in their homes. Energy suppliers need to be prepared, so they have enough energy to meet everyone's needs.

Safety

Many people look at weather forecasts to see if it will be safe for them to do something. Flying, sailing, and mountain climbing can be dangerous in high winds, heavy rain, and low cloud. If the forecast shows that this sort of weather is likely, pilots, climbers, and sailors may decide not to go out until the bad weather clears.

■ *If ice-cream sellers know the forecast is for hot, sunny weather they will make sure they have plenty of ice cream.*

Disasters

Disasters are caused by extreme weather conditions. Heavy rain, high winds, and storms can cause chaos. High winds often cause damage to buildings. After heavy rain, rivers can burst their banks and flood towns and villages. Floods damage people's homes and businesses. There is also a risk of people drowning. In extremely cold weather, roads and railways can freeze up and accidents are more common.

■ *Predicting the weather gives **meteorologists** time to give out warnings of floods and storms. If the people in Carlisle had been warned of this flood in January 2005, they might have taken preventative action, such as moving their furniture upstairs, or moving out of the area for a few days.*

Exploring further

Go to the Heinemann Explore website or CD-ROM, click on Resources > Weather. Now watch the video on flooding in Greece. Think about the kind of damage a flood like this causes, and what the people could have done if they had known about the flood in advance.

What will the weather be like today or tomorrow, here and around the world?

If you look out of the window or go outside, you can clearly see what the weather is like at this moment. If you want to know what it will be like in the future, you need to see or hear a **weather forecast**. We can get the weather forecast from several **sources**.

Television

The weather forecaster on television usually begins with the forecast at that particular time for the country you are in. They then say how the weather will change over the next few hours. Forecasters often finish by **predicting** the weather for the next day.

■ *The weather forecast can help you to plan what you are going to do or what you are going to wear*

Radio

There are usually regular weather reports on the radio. They often come just after the news reports. Like television forecasts, they give information about the current weather and predict the weather for the following day. Radio also broadcasts the very accurate **shipping forecasts** that give precise weather details for particular sea and coastal areas.

Newspapers

Daily newspapers usually have information about the weather. In a local newspaper this might be only about your local area. In a national newspaper the information will cover each main area of the country. It usually also has information about the weather in other countries, such as the **temperature** in major cities around the world. There is also usually a forecast of tomorrow's weather, and maps showing weather symbols.

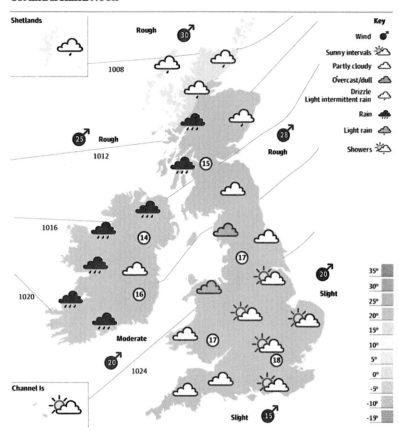

A weather report from a newspaper.

Internet

Many websites give weather forecasts for today and tomorrow. A good example is at: http://ukie.accuweather.com/adcbin/ukie/index.asp. Click on 'world' in the lefthand menu and you will see an interactive map. As the Internet allows you to search for information from all over the world, you can look at local weather reports from different countries to find out what the weather is like there.

Some websites have **webcams** that allow you to see the weather in different places. There is one placed in Cardiff Bay, so wherever you are in the world you can see for yourself what the weather is like there.

Activity

1 Look on the Internet to find the weather forecast for your area today.
2 Now find the weather forecast for Beijing in China.
3 Compare the two forecasts. Suggest reasons for any differences.

23

Media data

How do we analyse media data?

We use many different types of **media** to collect geographical **data**. They include newspapers and magazines, television, radio, and the Internet.

■ *Television is just one type of media.*

Some geographical data that we get from the media is more accurate than others. Before we can use the data, we need to **analyse** it to make sure it is as accurate as possible.

Research

Information in books, newspapers, and magazines, and on the news has been well researched. **Journalists** must check that their facts are correct but people do get things wrong. Although you have heard something on the news, or read it in a newspaper, it may not necessarily be true.

Information on the Internet, especially, may not always be accurate. There are no rules about what people can include on their web pages. Always check the facts you read there to make sure they are correct.

- A web page produced by a well-known organization, such as National Geographic, is likely to be factually correct.

An unbiased report

When a journalist writes a news report they have to make sure their own opinion is not included. This is called writing an **unbiased** report. They may not agree with the topic they are writing about, but they must not let the person who is reading or listening to the report know this. This can be difficult if they feel strongly about the topic.

Activity

1 Read a report in a national newspaper that is related to geography. It could be about the weather or a traffic problem, for example.
2 Find another newspaper report on the same issue.
3 Compare your two reports with a TV report on the same subject.
4 List the facts common to each report. Did one contain opinion as well as fact?

Comparing sources

One way to check the data you have collected is to compare the same information from different **sources**. For example, if you are collecting data about the height of a mountain, a book might give you one figure but a website might give you a different one. To find the correct answer look at more books, magazines, or websites, and use the information that is the most **common**.

Exploring further

Go to the Heinemann Explore website or CD-ROM, click on Resources >Media. Now watch the video of a tornado and a hurricane. Think about how the media can help us communicate data on extreme weather events.

What is in the newspapers today?

Newspapers are a good source of information on what is happening in the world today. There are several types of newspaper. Each type includes different kinds of information.

Local newspapers

Local newspapers mainly have news and events about your area. People place advertisements in local newspapers if they want to buy or sell an item. Businesses also advertise their services in local newspapers.

Rain fails to dampen show spirits

| by Sophia Jay |

THOUSANDS braved torrential rain to attend what is now officially known as Thame and Oxfordshire County Show 2005.

But the mudbath was not enough to dampen the spirits of those who turned out to trade, exhibit and enjoy.

This year's main attraction, on top of the ever popular agricultural, showjumping and dog classes, were The Knights of Arkley, who brought the medieval art of jousting back to life before the eyes of a dazzled audience.

Other crowd-pullers included The Band of the Prince of Wales Division (Lucknow), Thame Concert Band and the usual array of flower, vegetable and domestic produce classes.

In his speech show president, Lord Hollenden, a descendant of Thame's most famous rebel, John Hampden, warmly welcomed people to the 138th show, adding: "It is impossible to underestimate the importance of events such as the Thame Show. A recent local survey showed that an overwhelming majority of farmers in this region felt that increasing public awareness of farming and rural issues was of primary importance to them.

"The Thame Show fulfils that criteria in a unique and highly enjoyable way. People from all walks of life, from both town and country, genuinely look forward to their day at the show."

Chairman, Andrew Duffy, added: "We have tried a few different things this year including a farmers' market. We also have a lot of new motor dealers for which we are very grateful."

Show secretary, Mike Howes, was delighted that the rain did not seem to have affected attendance levels. He said: "The weather is unfortunate but it doesn't seem to have put people off. Although I do not have the official figures yet, the gates looked very promising.

"We have had a superb entry of cattle and sheep, and everybody seems to be in good spirits, despite the weather."

Perhaps the biggest smiles were on the faces of the show's most prestigious award winners. The Countryperson of the Year Award went to Chilton farmer, Bill Cooper, whilst Brian Gill, also of Chilton, scooped the Long Service Award.

Mr Cooper, who in more than 30 years of working for Aubrey-Fletcher Estates, has built up a range of agricultural skills, which have made him famous in his community, was delighted with his award.

He said: "I think it's champion, and an unexpected honour - though I wouldn't know if I deserved it."

Mr Gill, whose 30 years of work for R.H. Mole on Wurtenburg Farm included working with the farm's quality beef cattle, retired last autumn. He said: "I feel very honoured to have won this award

The wet weather obviously didn't dampen the enthusiasm of these young visitors to the show

Three-year-old   is delighted with the animals on show

Delighted: Long Service Award went to Brian Gill, of Chilton

- *News stories in local newspapers are about subjects that may seem unimportant to you, but which local people are interested in.*

Evening newspapers

Some newspapers are published in the evening instead of the morning. They report on events that have happened during the day. They are therefore very up to date.

■ *People catch up on the news on their way to and from work.*

National newspapers

National newspapers cover important events from all over the country and all around the world. Some have pages that are only about sport, business, or education. All have a section with a **weather forecast** for the whole country.

Activity

1 Look at some national newspapers and choose four national stories from them. Try to pick stories which have something to do with geography.

2 Use a map of the UK to locate the places where the news is happening. Label the places on the map and write a sentence to explain each story.

3 Write a short newspaper report on an event that has happened at school recently. Remember to keep it **unbiased**. Make up a headline that will attract the reader's attention. You could even include photographs, **statistics**, or maps if they are appropriate.

Weekend newspapers

Many of the national newspapers produce special editions on Saturdays and Sundays. These offer a huge range of information, often with a summary of the whole week's events. These newspapers can contain helpful geographical **data**. The sections about travel often have lots of geographical data, as well as descriptive photographs and information on the weather.

Communicating your data

Using email

The quickest way to get in touch with someone is to use the telephone. Sometimes you may want to send someone a written letter or some photographs. For this the best method to use is email, as long as the other person has access to a computer.

■ *Sending a document by email is very quick. A letter posted to someone on the other side of the world can take weeks to arrive. Emails can be sent all over the world in minutes.*

Style

Emails are written using a word-processing package, and can be as long or short as you like. You can also send extra pages, photographs, video clips, and pictures by email. Email is an excellent way of telling a link school or twin town about how and where you live – in other words your geography.

Activity

What would you do if you needed to get in touch with someone? Would you pick up the phone, write a letter or email them?

1 Ask your friends and family if they use email to communicate with others. If they do, ask them what they use it for and why they use email instead of other methods.

2 Record your results in an appropriate chart or **graph**.

Fax machines

Fax is the shortened word for facsimile. A facsimile is an exact copy of something. Fax machines send copies of written or drawn documents by electronic scanning. The copy is sent from one machine to another down a telephone line.

Most offices and schools have a fax machine, as well as a telephone and computers. Fax machines are useful when you want to send someone a hand-written message or a picture that someone has drawn. To send a fax to someone you need their fax number, which is similar to a telephone number. Faxes can be sent all over the world, and arrive much quicker than a posted letter.

■ *Modern fax machines can send faxes quickly. This means they are not connected to the telephone for very long, and so faxes are a cheap way to communicate.*

See for yourself

Ask your teacher to show you how the fax machine in the school office works. Many schools are linked to distant schools by fax. They use it to exchange news and information about their local area, for example comparing the weather.

Glossary

air pressure how hard the air is pressing against the Earth's surface

analyse to think about something in order to understand it

atlas book of maps

bar chart chart divided into columns to display data

calculations sums that give you an answer

capital city a country's most important city. It is usually where the government is based.

census set of questions sent to all adults in the UK every ten years

climate map map showing the climate of a region

common shared by several sources

data collected facts or information

drought when it does not rain for more than ten days

erode wear away rocks and soil by wind, water or ice

government the group people in charge of a country

graph visual display of data

grid squares squares on maps labelled with numbers and letters so that you can find a place easily

humidity how much water vapour is in the air

key symbols that are used on a map

line graph graph where the data results are joined up by a line

media sources of information, such as newspapers and magazines, television, radio, and the Internet

meteorologist person who studies the weather

model typical pattern of events in, for example, the weather

navigation using maps to find your way around

observing looking at something to obtain information

pattern predictable and recurring order of events

physical map map showing the physical features of the land

pie chart a round diagram divided into pieces, showing how an amount is split up

political map map showing countries, cities, and towns

predict to estimate what may happen in the future

radar system that uses radio waves to find the position of objects you cannot see

rain gauge instrument for collecting and measuring rainfall

satellite photograph picture taken from space

scale measurement on a map that shows how much land is shown

shipping forecast weather forecast for ships giving the conditions at sea

source place where you find out information, such as books, magazines, or websites

statistics the science of collecting and analysing data

statistician person who studies statistics to get useful information from collected data

survey asking people questions to collect information

temperature how hot or cold something is

thermometer instrument that records temperature

unbiased not affected by the writer's opinion

weather forecast report estimating what the weather will be like in the future

weather station place where weather data is recorded

webcam camera whose live film is displayed on the Internet

Find out more

Books

Mapping the UK: Mapping Coasts, Mapping mountains, mapping rivers, Mapping settlements, Louise Spilsbury (Heinemann Library, 2005)

Measuring the weather: Forecasting the weather, Allan Rodgers and Angella Strelluk (Heinemann Library, 2002)

Websites

www.nationalstatistics.gov.uk
Visit the government's official site for UK statistics.

www.heinemannexplore.com
Take a look at the Heinemann Explore website's Analysing Data section. The resources section contains videos and maps that help to bring the study of data to life.

Index

analysing data
mapping data 14–15
media data 24–25
photographic data 16–17
statistical data 4, 6–7
weather data 18–19
atlases 4, 12

census 4, 10
charts 5, 7, 8, 18
bar charts 8
pie charts 9
sea and air maps 13
communicating data 8–9,
   28–29
computers 18
counting 5

disasters 17, 21

email 28

fax machines 29
football league tables 11

geographical data 4, 24, 27
government statistics 10
graphs 7, 8
line graphs 9

Internet 23, 24, 25

mapping data 4, 12–15
analysing 14–15
atlases 4, 12
charts (sea and air maps) 13,
   14
climate maps 14

grid squares 12
key 12
Ordnance Survey maps 15
physical maps 14
political maps 14
scale 12, 14, 15
weather maps 23
media data 24–27
meteorologists 18, 19, 21
models 18

newspapers 11, 23, 24, 25,
   26–27

observing 5

patterns 6, 7, 8
photographic data 4, 16–17
analysing 16–17
satellite photographs 16
still photographs 16
plotting data 7
predictions 7, 18, 19, 20, 22,
   23, 27

questions, asking 4

shipping forecasts 22
sources, comparing 25
statistical data 4–11
analysing 4, 6–7
collecting 4–5
communicating 8–9
patterns 6, 7, 8
using 10–11
statisticians 6
surveys 10

television and radio 22, 24

unbiased reports 25
using data
statistical data 10-11
weather data 20–21

weather data 18–23
analysis 18–19
using 20–21
weather forecasts 18, 19, 20,
   22, 23, 27
webcams 23

Titles in the *Explore Geography* series include:

Hardback   0 431 03293 9

Hardback   0 431 03254 8

Hardback   0 431 03257 2

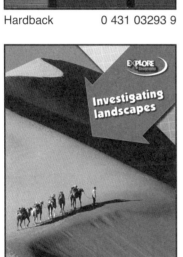

Hardback   0 431 03252 1

Hardback   0 431 03251 3

Hardback   0 431 03253 X

Hardback   0 431 03256 4

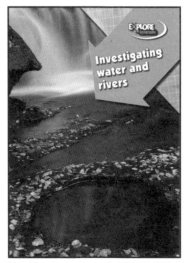

Hardback   0 431 03255 6

Find out about other titles from Heinemann Library on our website www.heinemann.co.uk/library